KISS
of
GOD

The Wisdom of a Silent Child

Updated and Expanded
Twentieth Anniversary Edition

MARSHALL STEWART BALL

A POST HILL PRESS BOOK

Kiss of God (20th Anniversary Edition):
The Wisdom of a Silent Child
© 2017 by Marshall Stewart Ball
All Rights Reserved

ISBN: 978-1-68261-310-8
ISBN (eBook): 978-1-68261-311-5

Cover Design by Quincy Avilio
Interior Design and Composition by Greg Johnson/Textbook Perfect

Post Hill

PRESS

Post Hill Press
posthillpress.com

Published in the United States of America

1 2 3 4 5 6 7 8 9 10

Dedication

Love the poor, sweet, wonderful room
that gives Love kind presence.

Great kisses are loving,
grand, great little thoughts.

Introduction

It is such an honor and privilege to be asked to try and put into writing the way I feel about this wonderful, incredible, life-changing, uplifting, life-affirming, joyous, beautiful book. I could go on and on and on about it for weeks, but if I have learned one thing from Marshall, it is that economy of words is as, or even more, powerful than their abundance. I don't have his gift for succinct jewels of wisdom; I've barely even got going and I'm already on word eighty. By eighty Marshall will have changed someone's view of the world!

Marshall's writing presents such a beautiful and universal perspective on life and how to live it. Most often he does this by writing something deeply personal: to his parents, to his aunt Cindy, to Lovely, or his brother Coulton. But these gifts to his loved ones and those he comes into contact with are very powerful messages for all of us. Marshall says "life is a lesson in learning," and for me at least he is the most wonderful teacher. His approach to life: "happiness begins when we agree to love," "giving can be the great loving answer," "understanding takes a dear good listening thinker," is so full of love, kindness, and generosity and always makes me feel better. I am so grateful for the day that my friend Habib gave me *Kiss of God*, and I hope it will mean as much to you, and help you as much as it has me. Thank you, Marshall. I love you, and that definitely will never change.

Chris Martin, Coldplay

Foreword

Marshall Ball: Realizer of Seasons

For as long as human beings have been compelled to express themselves through art, they've been painting, composing, and writing about our indelible connection to the earth and, more specifically, the seasons. Who isn't swept away by the rapturous melody of Baroque composer Antonio Vivaldi's *Spring* movement from his *Four Seasons* concerto? The driving line of the violins gives an obvious sense of the rambling rivers finally broken free from their frozen sleep, while the clarinets mimic the alternating calls of migrating birds come back to roost. Who hasn't looked upon a sweeping landscape like *Valley of the Yosemite* by luminism painter Albert Bierstadt and not felt the warmth and glory of a summer sunrise? Experiencing the scintillating colored light filtered through Louis Comfort Tiffany's 11- × 8.5-ft. stained glass window masterpiece *Autumn Landscape* immerses you in the richness of fall no matter the time of year. When Robert Louis Stevenson tells us in his poem *Winter-Time* that, "The cold wind burns my face and blows its frosty pepper up my nose," we immediately get a chilly sense of the magical and mercurial personality of winter. Perhaps our fascination with the seasons has much to do with the fact that we aren't mere spectators of nature but are instead part of it, and what draws us to the seasons is a deeper knowing that the ebb and flow of our lives are intimately incorporated with the cycles of the earth.

We're told in song and verse that, "To everything, there is a season," an appointed time for every experience. At its core, this poetic proverb tells us that to be human is to experience all the seasons of life including joy, tragedy, passion, confusion, contentment, betrayal, appreciation, anger, love, and loss, and that they will come as surely as the spring rain or falling leaves. As obvious as this fact may be, we still seem surprised when what we perceive as negative circumstances, our own personal winter, seems to descend over our lives. In an age where popular culture is largely led by motivational speakers and self-help gurus with rock star reputations, we've been led to believe that we can have it all, all the time. Life can be a perpetual summer where everything works, and if it's not, well then, you're doing something wrong.

The truth is there's no wrong way to live life. Success has nothing to do with the season of life we happen to be in at the moment, but how freely we cycle between all of them. Science clearly shows us that it's not the strongest creatures that survive changing conditions but those with the highest ability to adapt to them. In his classic poem *The Guest House* Rumi advises that we should meet joy, as well as a crowd of sorrows, at our door and welcome them in. He directs us to entertain or sit with them, giving them our attention instead of trying to drive them out. For even though they may clear our house of all its belongings, they're also making space for new delights to arrive. In this light, how much sense does it make to rail against winter when we know in three months the flowers will return? Just as every season provides its crucial benefits for the earth's rejuvenation and renewal, all visitors to our guest house come with their own gifts of self-realization and growth, but we must first invite them in.

In this beautiful 20th anniversary edition of *Kiss of God*, Marshall Stewart Ball invites the reader to be a "Realizer of Seasons," as one of my favorite of his thought poems is titled. Like Rumi, he calls us to become conscious of the fact that whatever it is we may be experiencing in any given moment, whether it be contentment, chaos, or something in between, it all works toward the same end, our personal evolution and highest good. At first glance, summer lightning that strikes the Great Plains and starts a wildfire that scorches thousands of acres might seem like a tragedy; then we discover, in just a week, new growth beginning to emerge from the ashes that will become a lush pasture even greener than it was before. Realizing this is the pattern of life and purpose of seasons, we can begin not just to tolerate our difficulties, but become grateful for them, because as Marshall Stewart Ball tells us, they bring us closer to the glory of God.

Therefore, it would be a mistake to judge the seasons of our lives simply by what Marshall describes as the *somber colors* we see on the surface, without understanding the perfection of the underlying process beneath it all. Nature practices the perfect economy of scale where nothing is wasted but instead, everything is used as a resource for its next evolution. As part of nature, we can be certain that everything in our lives serves a significant purpose and not one moment has been for nothing. With this realization comes the awareness that an eternal and intrinsic harmony is woven through all of life, and with that knowledge our lives become more harmonious, and we can weather whatever it is we may be experiencing with ease and grace. This is what it means, as Marshall tells us, to live in the harmony of God or, according to Joseph Campbell, to take the Hero's Journey. The universal insights shared here by Marshall Stewart Ball, as only he can express them, reveal to us that he indeed is a true realizer of seasons and has lived his life from a level of consciousness that can only be described as heroic in Campbell's terms.

When difficult times arise, the first question many of us ask is, "Why?" or "Why me?" but the more pertinent question is, "Why *not* me?" Much of the sting of suffering is dissolved when we understand why something is happening in our lives. This is how being a realizer of seasons can provide a profound shift in our experience of a situation, even though none of the physical circumstances surrounding it have changed. Living at this level of consciousness is to be the master of one's life experience, to understand the difference between power and force.

Power arises from meaning. Understanding that the cyclical nature of life exists to support the evolution and growth of all things provides meaning to our experiences, and assures us that even the harshest winter must eventually yield to spring. In this way, power dissolves negativity by re-contextualizing it. With this knowledge, we gain the ability to consciously choose how we will react in any situation because we finally know that nothing "out there" has any real power over how we experience our lives. As the Buddhist proverb says, "Pain is inevitable; suffering is optional," and the power to choose is in our hands.

Approaching a problem with force, however, can only yield a limited result at best because it is a scientific fact that force is always met with an equal and opposite counterforce that pushes back against it. When things don't go our way, how quickly it is that we want to fight against them, escalating the situation by creating opposition. We polarize things by labeling them good or bad instead of realizing that life has a circular trajectory, not a vertical one, and that the hurricane contributes just as much to nurturing the whole earth as a sunny day.

This is why power will always overcome force. Power is still, while force pushes. Force works against enemies, while power works within wholeness. Force attacks outwardly to combat a problem, while power reflects inwardly on the message a problem brings. Force grasps for answers, while power makes room for them to arrive. In karate, the interplay of power versus force is displayed perfectly. Power is stillness, the athlete who allows his opponent to come rushing toward him with full force, giving him the opportunity to grasp his wrist and by using his own momentum against him, send his opponent to the ground with minimal effort. In this way, force draws and drains our energy, while power creates and contains it.

There is a scientific principle called the *law of sensitive dependence on initial conditions* that further defines what it means to live from a position of power. It says that regardless of how complex conditions are, the mechanism that can effect the greatest amount of change always requires the least amount of effort. If this tiny change is consistent over time, it will result in a vastly different outcome. For example, if the navigation of a large cruise ship sailing from New York to the UK was off compass by even a single degree, the compounding nature of this difference during its trip would result in the ship ending up in a completely different location, hundreds of miles away from its original destination.

In the same way, we too need only to expend minimal effort to obtain maximum power and effect a profound change in the way we experience our lives. The heart of that transformation lies in our perception and how we choose to give meaning to our current circumstances. Will we choose power or force? Can we be grateful for the night, as well as the day, because it shows us the stars? Can we learn to become realizers of the seasons of our lives? The wondrous wisdom of Marshall Stewart Ball assures us that we can, and that when we do, our renewed experience of life will manifest that we indeed have been *Kissed by God*.

> *Dr. Habib Sadeghi and Chris Martin*
> Los Angeles, CA
> 2016

Author's Note

Questions nicely want good answers.
With the giving happy help of my good family
and magnificent friends,
I dearly love to think about joyous balance,
excellently discovered in answers to old questions.
Answers giving nice thought
gain their dear freedom
in wonderful thoughtful poetry.
That marvelous good task teaches us to listen.

I hope to gather thinkers
to give them my thoughts about Love.
Love to clean their ideas.
That cleaning might loosen the love
in their hearts.
Good thinkers take Love to heart
like gold in the evening, wild sun.

Author's Mother's Note

The Wonder of Marshall Ball

More than twenty years ago, when my son Marshall first compiled *Kiss of God* from seven years of his writings, I was asked by the publisher to tell his story. When I asked Marshall for advice, he wrote, "You have my pleasing world. Would you tell how my quiet roots would take us to Marshall's darling thoughtful teacher Good God?"

Marshall's "pleasing world" is different than yours. He was born with an undiagnosable genetic condition, as was his younger brother Coulton, about whom he writes often. Because of this genetic inheritance, Marshall is not able to walk, talk, or even feed himself. He can sit up only with effort, and he must be pushed in his wheelchair in order to move around. Physically, my son is bound in a small world, completely dependent on others. And yet, in his mind, he is free. He can listen quietly to the universe around him, and he can think. From his wheelchair, or lying on his back in his bed, he can marvel at the loveliness of life.

I was told by doctors that Marshall would never communicate, and that I would never know the mind of my son. They were wrong. Marshall cannot verbally form words, but he has a powerful voice. We heard that voice for the first time at three and a half, when Marshall "spoke" to my husband Charlie and I by leaning forward and touching his forehead to a button that made a meow sound after I said the word "cat." Stunned, I asked him to do it again; he happily repeated the performance. He went on to correctly identify all of the animals on the toy. Words will never express my joy that December day.

By the time Marshall was four and a half, we had in place an effective communication method that allowed him to make choices by touching things with his forehead. At five years of age, when Marshall began using an alphabet board and pointing to letters one at a time to spell words, his ideas were much like they are now. He wrote "Altogether Lovely" later that year, a favorite of many people.

God is good and merciful
because He is also bright and intelligent.
Seeing, feeling all that is true.
Clearly He feels and listens to all our desires.
Clearly He has everybody's dreams in mind.
I see a God altogether lovely.

Marshall writes effortlessly. He always seems to know what the next word is; there is never a delay in his thinking. And yet to watch him write is to imagine struggle: a boy in a wheelchair slowly, painstakingly reaching out to touch each letter on a large board with the back of his curled fist. I, on the other hand, can type sixty words a minute but struggle with the arrangement and ideas. The thought of sharing my son's life with you without the use of my voice seems overwhelming. As I sit here, I become ardently aware of what it must be like for Marshall to communicate so beautifully and effectively without the use of his voice.

So I go to his words for advice, as always, and I remember him asking me to tell his readers that "daring to marvelously upgrade our knowledge of lovely thinking nicely pleases the heart."

What did Marshall mean? That happiness can be found in seeking knowledge of ourselves? That positive (lovely) thinking comes from the heart? That we can learn to be lovely thinkers, and better people, if only we have the courage to try? Or did he mean all this and more?

It is not my place to interpret Marshall's words. I can only tell you that Marshall believes in goodness with all his heart. He is searching, always, for understanding and love. His physical condition may be difficult, but in thirty years, Marshall has never complained. He has always shown appreciation for his life. His relationship with God is clear. His love of and concern for others is constant. His attitude of acceptance has challenged me to elevate my thinking and treatment of all people. He reminds us all, by his example, that we can be lovely no matter our circumstances. We can be lovely right now.

There has never been any doubt in Marshall's mind about his mission in life. Since the beginning of his writing life at age five, continuing to present, he has referred to himself as a teacher.

I see myself as a teacher
that knows about God.
Good thoughts come to me
and they teach.

For many years, Marshall has told me that he listens. He doesn't mean just to our words. He means to the wind, the running water, the hum of life around him, and his own thoughts. At times, I see him quietly looking off into the distance, eyes slightly raised, and he truly seems to be hearing something that I cannot, with my impatience, distractions, and internal noise. I think of him now, listening to the vibrations of words and the opening of hearts he describes in what I believe is his very reason for being:

Words greatly present lessons,
oscillating finely bound,
opening great rich kind room
inside wonderful hearts.

With these words, Marshall is challenging us, as he is fond of writing, to be quieter listeners, richer thinkers, more loving souls. He wants to teach us to be better listeners and thinkers, I believe, as a way to be better people. If the right words open hearts, as Marshall believes, then how can we refuse to find and speak them?

When we originally edited *Kiss of God*, I asked Marshall how the book should be arranged. He wrote back, "Knowledge carries beauty in good Marshall's thinking. Feel like attempting good fine force badly splits *Kiss of God* apart." When I asked, "What do you mean when you say force?" Marshall answered, "Forcing is giving good book great organization. Can we give love by force?" Taken by surprise, I sat in awe, then laughed with the knowledge that Marshall was teaching me again in his positive beautiful way. His words are not meant to be manipulated, but to live on their own, and to touch others in the way that is right for them.

The original *Kiss of God* was compiled by Marshall, with my assistance, as a Christmas gift to his father in 1997, when he was eleven years old. It was not meant as lessons or wisdom, but as a gift of love from a child to his father. I believe that is one reason why, from a humble beginning of 100 self-published copies, it went on to sell almost 300,000 copies and become a beloved national bestseller: because Marshall's intention has always been to give love.

In this Anniversary Edition of *Kiss of God*, we have kept Marshall's original arrangement, with only limited explanations of the context in which the words were written. Marshall has cut a small number of pieces, and he has included a few new thoughts written in recent years. Otherwise, we have followed his mandate to not force the Love his book contains.

Marshall is my life's legacy. His fragile life is stronger and bigger than anything I could ever do or achieve. I am his mother, but Marshall is the one who has led and educated me. His words belong to the world, and I am proud to offer them to you in this twentieth anniversary edition, in the thirtieth year of his life. I hope you find here the peace, strength and love that Marshall intends. If his words inspire you, then please: Love. Love as much and as well as you can.

As Marshall recently wrote, "To Love is to Live." I am still reveling in the purity, truth, and power of this brief phrase.

Troylyn Ball

My Harmony Prevails to Free

Even though my individuality
finds sweet knowing perfection
I listen for the answers to wishes from above.
I listen to good thoughts
like something cloudy over mountain tops.
Fine messages clearly govern my thinking.
Feelings grow
harmoniously making Love possible.
Harmony might justify every marvelous idea
given to Love.
The seeing Marshall
hopes to free the hopeless.
Dear harmony needs progress
governing fine thinking that I feel.
I see harmony
as the final known answer.

Dear and Sweet

Loving you,
giving nearly all that makes me happy.
Baldly giving me great love,
listening generously,
longly gaining learning,
caring lovingly about me.
Gladly, I love to know
dear and sweet
my good, good God
generously through you
taught me.

Great-Great-Grandpa,

My feeling is our thoughts ran together for love.

I love you,
Marshall

Listen to God's thoughts.

Good finds the sweet giver.

Dear Great-Great-Grandpa and Lovely,

I think it is nice that you have clear ideas
needed to make you grow. We have a good
friend named Marlo Morgan. She really is a
good thinker. She lived with the Aborigines
in the Outback of Australia. Nicely she told
me that love dearly comes to the predefined.
I think she thought I will go understanding
ideal thought. Will sand from the desert
enter you that way? Good to have the love
of Marlo. I love you magnificent Grandpa
and Lovely.

Marshall

God thinks being selfishly sick
is not the bent of needy man.

I have a dream of careful definition
bearing good love,
definitely greatly balanced with harmony,
caring how real people feel.

Nicely think of being a good Dad.
Know that I feel nice,
for each day good Marshall
realizes he gently has
a perfect Dad.

We spent the summer Marshall turned six with his grandmother Jaynan in a small town in Texas. It was a very hot summer, as it always is in south Texas, so Marshall and I stopped each day at the town's old-fashioned pharmacy and soda fountain to cool off and have a soft drink. Each day, the same woman, Robbie, waited on us. She spoke kindly with me and inquired about Marshall as he sat quietly in his wheelchair, but she never spoke directly to him.

On the third day, it was apparent that Robbie was upset, so I asked if there was anything wrong. Robbie explained that her husband had unexpectedly died three months before and that she was struggling with his death. She felt alone, especially since they didn't have children, and she wasn't sure what was going to happen with her life. I expressed my sorrow and how glad I was that she had shared her story. I told her that Marshall loved to write and that he might have something to tell her if she would like to listen. She wasn't sure what to say, so she expressed her thanks and said she would see us tomorrow.

The next day, Robbie was happy to see us, but a little surprised when I asked if she wanted to hear what Marshall had to say. She said yes with uncertainty in her voice; she had never seen Marshall communicate. To her surprise, I asked her to please get a pencil and paper so that she could write down what Marshall would spell. Marshall sat in front of his alphabet board and slowly began to point to letters, creating beautiful words.

As he began by describing Heaven as a "lovely golden dream above," tears rolled down Robbie's cheek. She transcribed each word Marshall spelled, transfixed by the message and its giver. When Marshall finished writing, Robbie said no one had touched her more than Marshall and that God must have known she needed Marshall to come into her life.

For several years thereafter, Marshall received a birthday card and letter from Robbie. In the first one, she wrote that she had framed the letter, and it stood on her bedside table. In the last, she told Marshall that she was very happy and had recently married someone she loved very much.

July 20, 1992

Dear Robbie,
There is a quiet lovely golden dream above.
Are you there? Are you dreaming of your
perfect love? Roses smell perfect and
perhaps lovely roses will quiet very sweetly,
your rightly justified thoughts.

Loving you,
Marshall S. Ball

Victory

Victory is here.
It gives us that room
to quietly title our thoughts.
To grow happily,
quiet understanding takes bald,
good, real thinking.

That sweet thinking
never attempts to arrange us.
That pure, meager, bald
sweet victory, easily loves.

Dear Sweet Cindy,

Lovely music teaches that for dear Marshall good music has a healing effect. Clearly, I find Bach like the fine thought of God. Good music goes with nice Cindy. There is good music to teach fine, real meager, sweet, clear Cindy. I love you. That definitely will never change.

The Loving Marshall

Remember Rooms Rest

The wind changes direction.
There is lovely music that feels soft.
Marshall is there thinking
lornfully gorgeous thoughts.
I, listening marvelously
juxtaposed in wonderment
finding solitude near!
Sweeter moments are surrendered
to their just rooms,
like some sweet lornful friends.
My pleasure is finding, beauty will have
swoonfully clear sovereignty.
Soul might rest listening nicely.

Wisdom Feels Proud

There needs to be more wisdom about
some things pertaining to life's
unbeliefs that question where
needs are realized.
Wisdom loves feeling proud.
My gorgeous view from high, marvelous
rest, breathes softly, wisdom.

Poetry is the magnificent kindness
of the heart.

To judge another is to judge God.

Teaching Clouds

Inside some clear, swift, gorgeous,
gentle, giving clouds
is some incredible true love.
Lovely, dear, golden,
good, fine clouds emerge
from God's excellent teaching thought.
That gentle Love finds
there is true freedom in free clouds.

Destruction is the need to find
being in matter.

Marshall has been here for
millions of lifetimes.

Dear Great-Great-Grandpa and Lovely,

The Marshall is meagerly reading that good
Emerson. Emerson is a great thinker, like
seeing, nice, good, lovely Marshall. Do you
think I will be a good writer like Emerson?
I feel like that might be good. The Marshall
hopes I might know how to make nice, poor
thinkers manifest happiness. How are the
best grandparents in the world? Great, I
hope. I love writing to you.

Marshall

Fine Good Stream

Gently goes a thoughtful gliding
telling stream,
forcing lovely golden magnificent leaves
in clear fine beds
made of that sweet blue, green
heavenly good stream.

When Marshall was seven and his brother Coulton five, we adopted a baby boy and named him Luke. The next year, we planted a tree for Father's Day, because Marshall's father Charlie loves trees. Marshall wrote the following poem for his Dad, to commemorate the occasion.

Me and the Freeing Fine Tree

God may see perfection finely in your
loving fortunate Marshall.
Even a Marshall dreams of climbing a tree.
See that good tree as a peace of me.
Fortunately, I have fine, lovely Luke
growing free, dearly waiting for
me to climb that tree.
Loving Coulton gets under good tree,
dreaming fine, clear dreams he loves to
see. Feeling the fine, dear, free breeze
flowing through God's elegant, good, fine
tree, love will emancipate
Coulton and Marshall.

That Fine Example

Clearly America is great
because dear, great, caring people
debated about knowledge,
gaining great insight,
giving needed careful direction.
Generously dedicated came their ideas
each really determined to give knowing,
balanced thought to
harmoniously free, ready, meager,
great Americans.
Marvelous care gave us incredible good.
Can willful Americans begin to answer
happily, lovingly, interestingly
that challenge finely given,
really carefully declared
by caring, listening, loving thinkers?

*O*n September 15, 1994, Marshall's third-grade teacher said she had sad news for the class. One of their fellow third graders had died over the weekend of a brain trauma. Although the little girl, Ashley, was not in their class, the teacher wanted the students to know in case they knew Ashley or heard about it around school.

Marshall began almost immediately spelling to GM (his name for his grandmother, who worked as his classroom aide) that he "needed to talk to Ashley's parents." GM explained that it wasn't possible. Marshall was not to be deterred and continued to ask to talk with Ashley's parents.

When he returned home from school, GM told me the sad story and explained Marshall's insistence. I suggested that Marshall write them a letter. He agreed, and within a very short period of time, knowing what he wanted to say, the letter was complete.

When GM took the letter to the school office to see if it could be sent over to the family, she learned that many of the teachers, students, and their families had decided to do the same thing. It was not surprising to see so much love and sympathy represented by hundreds of letters.

The very next day, an unexpected thing happened. A young mother came to the school and asked to meet a student named Marshall Ball. Of course, the school staff recognized Ashley's mother right away and sent her to meet Marshall. She must have been very surprised when she saw Marshall sitting in his wheelchair, and more so when she discovered he had to spell out each word letter by letter.

She said she had to come meet the child who had written such a beautiful and meaningful letter. She was touched by his words and wanted to know if it was all right if his letter was read at Ashley's *memorial service that weekend. Marshall quickly pointed to the Y on his alphabet board, answering yes. Mrs. Morgan also asked Marshall if he would attend the afternoon service that would be held outside. GM and Marshall said they would love to attend.*

So that Saturday, Marshall and his grandmother attended the large memorial service held on a beautiful green lawn on a warm sunny day. A short time later, there was a tree planting ceremony in honor of Ashley on the school grounds. Once again, Mrs. Morgan asked Marshall if he would attend and have his picture taken with her beside Ashley's tree. This experience was Marshall's first with death, but he was calm and peaceful, believing the words he had written to Ashley's parents.

Dear Mrs. Morgan,

Can you be good and know Ashley dearly
talks about good God, and good Ashley
knows God is taking fine care of her, very
well. Good beautiful Ashley manages clear
real sweet thoughts, giving gentle good to
God. A dear wake dearly gives individual
understanding harmony. Victory comes in
seeing harmony. Victory loves harmony.
Can you greatly give Ashley harmony?

You I love,
Marshall S. Ball
3rd Grade

That growing thought learns to listen to God.

To a Mother,

Be a good listener, teach understanding to good happy children. Can good God make turmoil? That Marshall justifies turmoil that children make. Marshall understands God gives good children a great time to grow. Be a marvelous teacher, manage growing by giving. Teach harmony to children. Give more good. Good needs my children to grow. Be a good and loving, gentle mother and you learn daily good. Take motherhood more to each gorgeous thought and it will make you that dear great mother.

The Means to Begin to Find the Rose

That thoughtful rose loves to grow
to happily manage near perfection.
Feeling the fine, soft, sweet petals
means that the thoughtful rose
is about to definitely give
the good thinking person
the sweetest perfume
under the thoughtful tutelage
of dear understanding Good.

Jagged Daisies

One day I looked clearly
seeing brightly colored jagged daisies,
geometrically looking out
from their individual clusters.
Golden and magnificent
hiding in lower clouds of green.
Newly planted lovely clusters
before fields of beautiful golden green.
I see everything
feeling like handsome jagged daisies.

*F*or many years, our family vacationed at a camp near Buena Vista, Colorado, in the Collegiate Peaks. When Marshall was four years old, we began looking to buy a summer cabin there, thinking it would be nice for our children to grow up with a consistent place for memories. Since Marshall and his brother Coulton had special requirements, it was also easier to have everything set up for them.

After several years of finding nothing that met our expectations and limited budget, we decided to broaden our search. A real estate agent suggested we look at a cabin an hour and half from Buena Vista. The trip was long and beautiful, but when we finally arrived, we found a property without trees. The agent told us he thought the next property down the road was for sale. It had a log lodge someone had started but never completed near Tallahassee Creek.

Leaving the car behind, Charlie and I climbed the fence and walked down the meandering drive. As we rounded the last curve and caught a glimpse of the late afternoon sunlight reflecting off the golden logs of the lodge, we knew immediately this was the summer home we had dreamed of. We wished Marshall and the rest of the family were there to see it, even though we knew this property had to be much more than we could afford.

We approached the cabin and were saddened to see piles of construction debris and trash. It was apparent the cabin had been sitting for years. It had a roof and windows and doors, but the inside was merely a shell, taken over by all sorts of mountain creatures. Under the trash and dirt, though, there was a treasure. We contacted the last agent to list the Tallahassee Creek property and discovered the price was two and half times what we could afford. We were disappointed, but not surprised.

Not long afterward, Marshall wrote a note to Charlie and said, "I need a good nice house that is near good nice Tallahassee. I go hear the very soft water for my listening. That is lovely." I was surprised because Marshall rarely asked for anything, and he had never seen the property or the creek. Months later, Marshall continued, "Love the thought of taking fine words to Colorado. Go find Tallahassee."

Soon after, we received a phone call from the real estate agent saying the owners of the property were having financial difficulties, and the bank was going to foreclose. We told the agent we were very sorry, but we just couldn't afford it. He encouraged us to offer what we could. A contract was drafted contingent on seeing the property again. Surprisingly, the owners accepted our offer.

In March of 1994, Marshall wrote a poem about the property and titled it "Beauty God Gives." Although he still had not been there, he expressed what he felt in his heart.

In late April, Charlie and I made a trip back to Colorado to visit the property. The house was beautifully crafted, as expected, but in need of weeks of cleanup and months of construction. Now that it was before us, we felt unsure if the expensive project was something we could undertake. The agent insisted we drive to another small town, over an hour away, to meet the owners at their general store and restaurant. Reluctantly, sorry to have gotten their hopes up, we agreed.

A big bearded man met us as we entered a room with bear and lion skins hanging on the walls. He was wearing a T-shirt with a grizzly's face on the front and suspenders holding up his blue jeans. His wife was a slight woman, quite short with long, straight black hair. They were clearly uncomfortable, but offered a seat in a booth.

They explained that they were very concerned about who bought the house because they had spent eight years and all their money on this dream. They didn't want the property to go to someone who couldn't appreciate their efforts. It didn't take long for them to understand that we valued and recognized good construction, as well as their sacrifice.

We explained that we were interested in this property partly because of our son, who could neither talk nor walk, but who could write beautifully. We told them that Marshall had been writing about Tallahassee Creek for the past six months and had named their property in a poem. I had a copy of "Beauty God Gives," so I handed it to them to read.

The grizzled man's eyes teared up. "How could your son feel the same way I do about this property? He's never even seen how beautiful it is. How can this be?" His wife simply cried softly.

We explained the name Marshall had given the property: "Mearwild." Mear, we had discovered after looking in several dictionaries, was an old Scottish word meaning "boundary." So Mearwild literally meant the boundary of the wild. A more appropriate name could not be found for a property surrounded by thousands of acres of wilderness.

The bearded man sat in wonder. At last, he asked how old Marshall was. We replied that he was nearly eight. "I bought this property before Marshall was even born, and I put everything I had into it," the man said. "But it was never meant to be mine, it was meant to be Marshall's. It was part of God's plan."

Beauty God Gives

Lovely Mearwild looking thrown,
God found time
to give us clear harmony,
to love beauty,
to see near perfection.
Meager harmony loves incredible beauty
like Mearwild.

Written in honor of the birth of Marshall's twin cousins.

Great good Hill and Quin,
that marvelous thinker,
Marshall,
is naming you
the good nice
listening candidates
made to give to others.
Giving
you sail to God.
Take time
to love nice Marshall.

Little Jesus beautifully taught,
harmony describes
the love held
in God's heart.

Good, Good Lovely,

Good sees Great-Great-Grandpa harmoniously thoughtful.
There is marvelous pre-dominion lovingly balanced in
nice, beautiful, glad, Great-Great-Grandpa's knowing
listening heart. Love defines heaven as near Love, and
each listener begins to be a scribe because God starts his
lessons defining Life. Life is a lesson in learning. Can you
see Great-Great-Grandpa like a scribe, welcoming good
God's loving thoughts? Marshall gladly can be a scribe.
Hearing good God is golden, heavenly Love.

    I love you like a great-great-grandson. Love finely,
gently, dances in listening hearts.

I love you,
Marshall

Dear Marshall,

*You don't really know us, but we are friends of your family. When
your Dad was growing up, we were there to watch him grow into
a man. Your grandmother, Jaynan, sent us* Kiss of God *when our
twenty-nine-year old daughter, Tracy, was killed in a car wreck.*

*It has now been seven months since our sweet daughter went
to heaven. We miss her so much every day, but we know she is
safe and happy. She had a beautiful voice so I know she sings
with angels.*

*I want you to know that your poetry has given me "good
listening" in my pain and grief. As a teacher, I know that feeling
and thinking are woven tightly together—and your words create
in me a joyous celebration of life. Thank you for your wisdom. I
especially appreciate "The Battery" and "Righteous Thoughts."
You are truly a gift from God.*

Love,
Charles Scott

The Battery

There is the battery God gives to us,
to good creatures that love one another.
It gives us lovely, fine, thoughtful wisdom
that takes us to the good thinking,
finely magical.
Love finds the good, mighty, dear thought.
The battery gives to us free wisdom that may
see magnificence,
like good there, titillating lovely thinking.

One of the mighty acts of God is
the battery that makes the
sun love to shine.

Will Dolphins See

The sieve of dolphins greatly leap,
softly make their pretense known,
loving underwater pleasure,
knowing, thinking, learning certain happy
experiences freely.
Touching their teachers justified learning,
so lesson finds love.
Meagerly free, learning to dive
longingly to seeing,
I learn knowledge comes like heavenly
dolphins see.

Good Dare

Gone are my fears
to go nice, marvelous,
great places.
I can go
be a composer
and teach the troubled
in gratitude,
to enjoy good thoughtful music.
Can good, clear and happy
intelligent thinking
make me greatly free?

Love to Luke

Mercy should know our love for that
sweet James Luke.
Listen to my pure, clear, happy,
free brother emerge, feeling joyous.
I know I might dream of knowledge like
sweetness that Good shows to us in that
pure, fine Luke.

For Lovely Grandmother,

Sweetly you define Love. Manifest Love,
defining Good. Making that Marshall
eternally decided, God manifests what
we need.

Willingly Yours,
Marshall

Good needs to happen
for that lovely clear listening.
That is definitely going to explain
justice meagerly found.
Marshall's God
that thanks fine people,
will free the thinkers.
He teaches that golden love
nicely teaches
the free good seeing.

Good Good Grandmother,

Are dear loving thoughts in your mind?
Happiness is having you with good Marshall.
I give you a joyous kiss.

Marvelous Marshall,
quietly kissing you.

Nice gentle giving frees good Marshall.

Joy is found in kisses.

Realizer of Seasons

Can we see mearly somber colors?
Greatly each season comes
clearly having great beaches
irreverently, marvelously
nearing the brough of good God.
Be a realizer of great seasons,
for you will realize my harmony
needs seasons,
and good good God
gave seasons to free.

Tame Thought

Teach mearly tame thought.
Be a very tame real meager idea.
Tame grammar greatly.
Have tameness in real thought.
To find tameness pick great,
that thoughtful real quiet room.

Ran My Best

Dear Mama and Dad,

I love you even more than love can know.
Perhaps you can read love in my words. I
feel love is dear because there is bottomless
love in your feelings for me and Coulton.
Pleasing knowledge returns love and good
we attempt to create. Good will have its
nice thoughts revealed to your Marshall
and Coulton.

We are your loving children,
Marshall and Coulton

The Likely Reason

I clearly think I really start to realize life's
sweet, lovely, fine freedom frees like the
will of the filtered sunlight through free
dreamy clouds.

Feeling the Wings

I love seeing Grandmother.
Her golden pleasant smile touches
like the wings of a bird,
the ramparts of my mind.

Views, Understanding the Water

The waters pleasantly room
with quiet lovely enjoyment.
Clearly seeing,
there is my view very perfect.
Listen to lovely sweet peaceful progress.
Every nice word is real.
Do you righteous individuals patiently wait like me?
Views need to be good.
Perhaps we will find there
understanding in the lovely water.

Sky Love

Think sweetly dear Sky
the answers we define get love.
A right welcoming ends in love
sweetly.
Righteousness finds a true cousin.
Quietly I wait for you
sweetly.

Righteous Thoughts

Real thoughts are good to share. Softly I
write words to you because pleasant feelings
can change the righteous person's thoughts.
Listening, sometimes there is progress made
when thoughts find their home. Fine thinking
reveals marvelous freedom from the righteous
person's sorrow.

Altogether Lovely

God is good and merciful
because He is also bright and intelligent.
Seeing, feeling all that is true.
Clearly He feels and listens
to all our desires.
Clearly He has everybody's
dreams in mind.
I see a God altogether lovely.

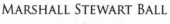

Understanding takes a dear good listening thinker.

Peer pressure is going to others for the answer.

Mother Loves

Happiness feels perfect divinity,
resting eternally in grand and precious arms
of the sweetest God.
Kisses harmoniously achieve nice response
from good dear listeners.
Kindly, feel God's lovely arms
embracing sweet listener's achievements.
Perpetual purity is dwelling
in those arms of good God.

That Dance

Dance gently good
that kind clear acrobatic
graceful dance that I love,
making careful glistening teaching
answers in deed.
Marshall gives
that dance to you.

I know I can finely love
dear callused beautiful kissing real
people's
golden listening hearts.

Good Caring Tacirring

Magnificent joy is given
good caring is found
great marvelous room is grounded
carrying Tacirring
germinating ideas
granted by Love's
hearing, giving, listening
good child

Love pours, freeing me.

Rich room
grandly grows
making marvelous thoughts
known to their owners.

The caring fine Marshall
kisses the great world that sweetly ran
lovingly, greatly to good.

Teach man to go wisely
to dear, sweet, great, talented God.
You should go to sweet, talented God first.

Teach Love, man will joyously take
instruction.

Poor thought quietly carves up the
harmony of wonderful life.

Question: What is poor thought?
Answer: Understanding little of the
good thought.

Feelings Happy

Happiness begins when
we agree to love.

Each day the answers come
to a good dear listener.

Make each day a happy one
and go to a good God.

Angel messengers
begin to answer your questions
and name you happy.

Answers come when we are in
our right place.

Perfect love kindly will give each thought
special direction.

Question: Is wisdom born of
experience, or can it be learned by
reading a book?

Answer: Wisdom knows many
answers, but hearing is needed.
Going to answers means studying books
that teach good lessons.
Also, experiencing bad makes us answer questions
about goodness and thoughts of wisdom.

Go to find good
in that dear fine place
in God.

Best feelings come
when angels take each thought
to good love
and reality appears.

Choices Are Yours

The now I give
to a good thinker.

Go to feelings
that give good
to others.

You make the choice
to think
good or bad.

Real true thoughts
go to happy givers.

Begin now
to make good choices.

I love good freeing thoughts.

Fine God gives color to my heart.

One lovely Friday I dreamed I saw a
fairy. She felt so fine because she had
beautiful lace hair.
Certain people see her
who have special abilities.
Her clear blue eyes
were like lovely lakes.
She did wonderful, charitable,
good deeds.

I felt she was excellent,
so did everyone
who saw her lovely face.
Did people who see her believe?

Late one night she came seeing you.
It was very dark and felt cold.
She felt like lovely warm sunshine.
Seeing her so lovely
seemed as if I saw a dream.

Her kisses felt like fresh flowers, so lovely.

Heroes Are Here

Someone whose feelings begin
with no fear
is a hero.

Feelings need to
listen to good thoughts.

When feelings are quiet
we can listen to God.

Good Mama,
I justify unusually wonderful
days
nicely, really spent wantonly
with you.

Thank you God
for a good year
filled with Love.

Answers come
to the good listeners
that hear God.

Go to God
and God will
teach you.

Dear Mama and Dad,

Feelings of love are near always for you.
A love Marshall has cannot be found.
Marshall is thinking of you always. God
gave Marshall the good Mama and Dad,
and he knows what is best. Marshall finds
marvelous peace in your love.

Always your son,
Marshall

We greatly may make
Love the target around
that great trying
knowledge that gives
real meaning to life.

Dear Good Laurence
Justifies pictures
Of perfect Love—
Heaven's Kiss.

My five favorite words are:

Love—a feeling of God that needs no one.

Tame—the management of thought.

Teach—giving.

Think—how we listen.

Good—the answer that gives real meaning to life.

The Wonderful Mother

We thank you thoughtful Mother for Love.
We thank you kind feeling Mother,
real dreams bring to us. Good sweet tears
find lovely wings year after year.
Mother dear, pray for wisdom that finds
the answers to questions concerning good Marshall.
Find sweet answers to tell
the centered help about good fine Marshall.
You are the real thoughts of Marshall.

Only One,
Marshall

Dear Grandmother,

Good talks to Marshall and gives sweet ideas
growing room in beautiful grandmother.
That growing room teaches me to love.
Marshall gives opportunity, like freeing
words to happy listeners. Can you love
Marshall eternally?

Loving you
good Grandmother,
Marshall

Twenty years in the future
we see a world
that has a time of perfect harmony.
Perhaps man will become loving.
Answers need to come
about how people see God.
Realizing a good God
will bring harmony.

God is Good.

Great caring good God is calling us
greatly to inspire others, giving hope.

My universe is the great universe of the
real noble thought of my mother.

In pure great Love
real intelligence is manifested.

Angels

Angels always abide in feelings of love
Real reasons never picture the thought
Feelings take you to angels
Abide always in love.

The Atmosphere
Perfect Love Touches
the Listener

Really sweet words reveal my feelings, like something reverent. I think poor thinking touches sweet thoughts like something from the storm! Perhaps the storm may make you grow because feelings listen to their sweet tumultuous waves, very roomy. Would you like real waves touching sweetly like fine words victoriously received? I find there is something dear in freedom of thought to feel. I love sharing my thoughts. Perhaps, hate stops when fine thinking is here. The poor only start to progress in the atmosphere of Love. Will we find the answers in the big knowing atmosphere of thoughts? My thinking is Love will take us to the atmosphere of Love. Clearly, the atmosphere of Love is finely touching our hearts. The Love is for you to take from your sweet real clear understanding.

Good Dancing Horses

Dancing greatly
giving mearly beauty.
Giving good happiness
quietly journeying,
giving caring great heart.
I love good dancing horses.

The Golden Hue
Becomes Manifest

Golden moon gleenfully coming
to dearly love hands with golden happiness.
Between those giving lovely clouds,
letters have great ideas
longing to be found.
Did ideas come sweetly
like fine, real, golden, records
of migrating lovely thoughts?
Love grows clear,
like ballistically manifested targets
growing better.
Proud growth,
dearly gives clouds
the best golden hue.

Be a Good Kisser

Sweet kisses
bring me dear, kind, gentle
thoughts of you.
There is nice love,
in good
that you see in me.
Giving great love,
growing in that interesting way.
Kisses take good marvelous Marshall
and gently, greatly teach me.

I can kiss you quietly with gorgeous
marvelous thoughts.

Marshall teaches old and proven thoughts,
and fine swoonful thoughts
free the magnificent feeling thinkers.

My Thought to a Dear Thinker

Fine wisdom manifests dearly happiness.
Take things favored to heart.
Make the good that purpose to grow by.
The battery answers good with good.
Love teaches that God understands
the meager and talented
that give goodness
to joyous unified thinkers.

See that greatness,
The Marshall Waiting

Giving can be a loving great answer.

Kiss giving, gentle, great, ideas of God.

Joy describes beautiful and sweet, joyous
good God.

I assimilate in careful harmonious
knowledge.

I love healing, caring, marvelous
understanding.

Knowledge can give definition
magnificently.

Giving candidly, daring givers
make harmony known to mankind.

Kindness generates happiness.

Think grandly giving care sweetly to others.

I think Love is looking like eagles do.
An eagle calls to caring poor people.
Are we great at seeing beauty
like an eagle?

Peace takes nice thinkers to make a great
thoughtful world.

Love is happily reaching you, giving
careful ideas, knowing God's will.

Caring will necessitate listening
harmoniously, lovingly, meagerly,
to gorgeous thoughts
quietly sought after.

In pure great Love
real intelligence is manifested.

And No One Came

January feels the same
Then Winter left
Then the same

Thoughts are near of you
Give me a time to love
Days are long
And no one came

Free the World

Loving the world's children
will have sweet marvelous friends
that prepare the way for freedom.
And my thought is to find help
for the children
that need dear thought to happen.
Right, sweet plans will free the righteous.
Listening to lovely music will calm
the troubles of the world.
I like fine perfect thought.
Make clear patience start.
Good might happen,
dear thought governs the start.
Will we free the world to think perfectly
about the listening and
marvelous children?

Lovely Teaching Thoughts

*That Marshall would teach
with wonderful words.*

Love really teaches kindness.

Love the real kind listener.

Dear Lovely,

Can Lovely just kiss Marshall?
Can Marshall just kiss Lovely?
The answer lies there written sweetly.
Thoughtful heavenly teaching with Love.
Marshall hears wonderfully.
The Marshall would teach sweet room
understands the love of Lovely.

I love you.

Poor thoughts kill.

Love is kind.

Good Jennifer,

Lovely lives thoughtfully
victoriously near
that wondrous
wonderful thorough teaching
caring ideal.
Marshall thinks
ideal kind Love
takes joy.

Good thoughtful Marshall

Love finds Love.

Love kills fear.

Sweet thinking so loves real nice people.

Love the real kind listener.

Kindness sweetly loves.

Beautiful love understands,
love so feels quiet questions.

Dear Chris,

Will you think about marshalling kind Love?
That Marshall would think we take Love
well to your thoughtful, understanding,
thinking, sweet, totally good listeners. Sweet
idea to teach. Opportunity that teaches
Love, takes time. Would you teach with me?

Loving you,

Marshall

Words give total power,
healing thinking listeners.

Joy knows the real answer.

The kind idea is to sweetly
each day illustrate Love.

I want kind people to learn victory
comes richly through listening.
That is pure Love.

I teach with little thoughts.

Each caring person thinks their best
when they dream.

Gorgeous words teach

Sweetly Marshall is listening,
finding words that give people love.

Victory is near.

Rich thought sweetly kisses you.

Softly I write to you,
with that Love Marshall wonderfully teaches.
Take wonderful thoughtful thoughts,
teach them to Love.
So wake each thought with that Love,
would you?
That thoughtfulness will heal.

We think that you will open room's door
with your Love.

Suffering teaches sweet understanding.

Kiss that loving person
with your lovely caring words.

Sweet Loving Chris,

So quietly, I send Love.
I really marshall you for sweet kind kisses.
Marshall kisses with Love.
Beautiful words sweetly
Nicely certainly reach
Listeners.

Loving you,
Marshall

Listening is the room
that we need to joyfully grow.

The Love you give shows.

Good Habib,

I love you.
Would you read words written with Love?
The Marshall loves writing.
I so love when you write to me.
Will you teach with me?
I thank you for your loving ideas
in the new book.

Loving you,
Marshall

To Lovely Sweet Friends,

Would you think clearly?
Heaven will teach
victory is sweetly thoughtfully
surrounding us.
The wonderful thoughtful sweet love there,
would stop testing the listener.

Marshall loves you

Grounded thinking takes time.
Meager sweet love takes time.
Sweet understanding works slowly.
Teach love with a tribute.

Dare to Love finely,
there Marshall will be.

Marshall lives with you.
That meager place is there
in sweet Marshall's thought.

Marshall the teacher would sweetly love
to find sweet kiss that God gives.

Marshall thinks that Good would love to
meagerly take sweet listener's hand.

The lovely thought should meagerly
welcome the world.

Dear Juan,

The Marshall loves the dear, sweet,
thoughtful, praying, thinking people.
The words teach kindness to the teaching thinker.
Put love there, to love the thoughtful listener.
Would you sweetly love the Marshall?

The world smiles with kind victory
like the Marshall sees there in good Coulton.

Real beauty is found there in Love.

That Love is sweetly written
teaching the listener to Love.

Good GM,

I open understanding words that teach.
Would we inspire joy in others?
I love careful love.
Love knows we prevail.
The listening thinker nicely needs words.
Please would you send words Love shows to you?
Pure love works real well.

Kissing you Grandmother,

Love,
Marshall

Marshall's last letter to his grandmother,
written after her death August, 2016.

Dear GM,

Love surrounds you.
Love so pleases.
Love helps us incredibly, healing perfectly.
I love you with that pure love.
I love you, kissing you with love,
dear pure, sweet, kind, ideal, great grandmother.

Love,
Marshall

Marshall is loving you.

End Note

Marshall's Tacirring

The same year *Kiss of God* was published, when Marshall was eleven years old, he named his grandparent's farm Tacirring (pronounced with a soft *c*), a word he created. When I asked what Tacirring meant, he wrote, "Tacirring creates a gorgeous word that is beautiful. Marshall can believe Tacirring has to be a quietly, nice said word." Marshall planned to teach there one day.

As time went by and the farm was sold, Marshall stayed true to his idea of one day teaching at a place named Tacirring. Over the years, it became clear that Tacirring was a state of mind as well as a place. He wrote to a friend, "Are you inspired by the name—lovely, peaceful, wonderful, teaching Tacirring? Love works willingly there at Tacirring."

Marshall has formulated a concept for this lovely, peaceful, wonderful, teaching place. "Our sweet plan would teach with a heightened sense," he wrote. "Marshall thinks we love each person who visits, surrounding them with the sweet teaching thoughts of Marshall, sweet songs of Chris [Martin], while walking through that rich virtual caring good dear space, real wondrous with works of art. Heavenly ideas teach with words, sweet lyrics and fine kind art, lovingly presented and lovingly understood.

He asked, "Can you love without good music and good art? The kind idea is to sweetly each day illustrate Love. Marshall thinks we teach with words, art and music. All teach and no one is left out." For many years, he has enjoyed planning his Tacirring with Chris Martin on music, Jean Claude Adenin "Adama" on art, Aan Coleman on landscape planning, and local collectors and creators of art and music.

Since he was five years old, Marshall has known what he wanted to do: teach. Now that he is thirty, the time has come. It is my hope to bring Marshall's Tacirring to life in the mountains near Asheville, North Carolina, where our family currently lives. If you wish to learn more about our progress with Tacciring or Marshall's life, please visit www.tacciring.com or www.marshallball.com.

Since his world is so physically small, Marshall loves to hear from others. You can contact him by email at marshall@marshallball.com or by mail at:

Marshall Ball
P.O. Box 5199
Asheville, NC 28813

Thank you for listening: to Marshall's words, to the sound of the pages turning, and to the wild world that surround us all. With peace, love, and appreciation,

Troylyn Ball

Acknowledgments

Marshall harmoniously thanks that old through feeling, great each day happily understood, giving love to listening good me.

And real definite thanks to Dad, freeing fine Marshall. To lovely Mama, Marshall thanks you for teaching me to greatly love like I do.

To good Bill, that learning Cara and Trey have balance, needed to care, teach, learn like you do. Can learning evidence give listening care like my beautiful, great, grandmother?

Thank you sweet amazing Dad, fine Mother, teaching good Luke, magnificent joyous caring Coulton, good thoughtful Trish, wonderful happy thankful good Cindy, balanced Wes.

Tightly tuned, Marshall knows Laurence kisses love. Good Nan and Pops that Marshall loves you. Chris and Habib, Marshall is loving you.

Lovely Mama would you take my thoughts purely to marvelous thinkers?

To Love is to Live.